For the real Mom, Dad, and Sandy

And Cathy East Dubowski,
an inspiring teacher

With love,
BG

How to Keep Your Helicopter

From the first time he twirled its propeller, Benjamin *loved* his toy helicopter.

He could do so many things with it.
He could pretend it was flying in the sky.

Pretend it was the mayor in a small town...

Or feed it a bowl of pasta.

Benjamin's sister, Sandy, saw how much fun he was having and...

She wanted a turn.

Now, normally, that wouldn't be a problem.
Normally, Benjamin was good at sharing.

But sometimes you just
don't want to share.

Benjamin's mommy was on the
telephone when she heard
Benjamin not wanting to share.

She had an idea.

"I'm going to teach you a trick," she said.
"A way that you can keep your
toy helicopter and make Sandy
happy at the same time!"

Benjamin was interested. After all,
he loved both of those things:

Keeping his toy helicopter

nd making Sandy
happy.

"How does this miracle solution work?" he asked.

"Well," his mommy replied, "You pretend like you actually want to be playing with a different toy."

"You see, it's not that Sandy wants to play with the toy helicopter."

"She wants to play with whatever you make look fun!"

Benjamin knew what he had to do. He had to make something he didn't really want to play with look just as fun as his helicopter.

He took a broom from the closet.

A broom was hardly a fun toy. It was something Benjamin's daddy used for cleaning the kitchen after dinner was over every night.

Benjamin brought the broom to Sandy,
and started to make it look like
the best thing in the world.

He rode it like a horse...

And used it like a sword...

And pretended he was a pirate
with a wooden leg.

Sandy wanted that broom.

But Benjamin had done such a good job convincing Sandy the broom was fun, he'd also convinced himself.

He was back to exactly where he started.
He had a great toy that he loved,
and Sandy wanted it.

Luckily, Benjamin's mommy knew lots of stuff, not just how to keep your helicopter.

She knew that while Benjamin
only had one helicopter...

His mommy and daddy had both
a broom *and* a mop!

"Hooray!" said Benjamin.
"Thank goodness for Mommy's trick!"

"Now everyone's happy!"

CPSIA information can be obtained at www.ICGtesting.com
Printed in the USA
LVOW02*0403180815

450293LV00025B/226/P